Big Bang
SCIENCE EXPERIMENTS

PUSH
and
PULL

THE SCIENCE OF FORCES

Jay Hawkins

WINDMILL
BOOKS

New York

Published in 2013 by Windmill Books, An Imprint of Rosen Publishing
29 East 21st Street, New York, NY 10010

First Edition

Editors: Joe Harris and Samantha Noonan
Illustrations: Andrew Painter
Step-by-Step Photography: Sally Henry and Trevor Cook
Science Consultant: Sean Connolly
Layout Design: Orwell Design

Picture Credits:
Cover: Monalyn Gracia/Corbis
Interiors: Ocean/Corbis: 4–5. Shutterstock: 21, 26.

Library of Congress Cataloging-in-Publication Data

Hawkins, Jay.
 Push and pull : the science of forces / by Jay Hawkins. — 1st ed.
     p. cm. — (Big bang science experiments)
 Includes index.
 ISBN 978-1-4777-0324-3 (library binding) — ISBN 978-1-4777-0368-7 (pbk.) — ISBN
978-1-4777-0369-4 (6-pack)
 1. Force and energy—Juvenile literature. 2. Friction—Juvenile literature. I. Title.
 QC73.4.H39 2013
 531'.6—dc23
                                                                2012026222

Printed in China

CPSIA Compliance Information: Batch #AW3102WM: For Further Information contact Windmill Books, New York, New York at 1-866-478-0556

SL002562US

CONTENTS

The force is strong in this book!

TOUCH THE SKY!

Skysurfers leap from planes with boards strapped to their feet. They don't just know about the science of forces: they live it! This book explores the same ideas through fun experiments.

RESISTING GRAVITY

Air resistance is a force that slows things down as they fall through the sky. Skysurfers can angle their boards to create more or less air resistance. They can't stop themselves falling, but they can control how they fall.

TERMINAL VELOCITY

At the beginning of a fall, skysurfers plunge through the air faster and faster as gravity acts on their weight, pulling them downward. Eventually, the resistance of the air balances their weight, and they stop accelerating. The fastest speed they can reach is called their terminal velocity.

RIDING THE CLOUDS

By tilting down the nose of his board, a skysurfer can create more air resistance at the back of the board than the front, pushing it forward through the air. By angling the board in other ways, he can use air resistance to perform twists and turns, and tricks like loops or helicopter spins.

BOOK BATTLE

This fantastic trick might seem like fiction, but actually it's all about friction!

Tell your friends, "I bet you can't pull these apart!"

Step 1

Take two big, thick books, with plenty of pages.

Step 2

Turn a page from each book alternately so that they overlap by a few inches.

Step 3

Continue until the books are completely combined.

Step 4

Find two volunteers, and ask them whether they think they can pull the books apart. It looks easy, but in fact it is impossible!

HOW DOES IT WORK?

When you slide two pages across each other, a force called friction resists the movement. When all the pages of a book are overlapped as in our experiment, that friction is multiplied by the number of pages. That's a lot of friction—so it's impossible for anyone to pull the books apart!

WEIRD WATER

This fiendishly clever bit of science can be used as a perfect practical joke to play on your friends and family!

YOU WILL NEED:
- ★ A plastic water bottle
- ★ Water
- ★ A thumbtack
- ★ An outdoor space—this could get messy!

Step 1

Fill a plastic water bottle right to the very top.

Step 2

Screw the cap on firmly.

"Water" great experiment!

Step 3

Make holes around the sides of the bottle with a thumbtack. The water won't come out—yet! Now take your bottle somewhere that you don't mind getting wet.

Step 4

Ask a friend if they would like a drink, and give them the bottle.

Step 5

When they open the lid… the water will pour out of the holes. They're in for a soaking!

Now try this:

Try doing the same experiment with a soft-sided container, like a large plastic bag. Fill the bag with water, hold it up with one hand, and make holes with the thumbtack.

HOW DOES IT WORK?

Water cannot escape through the holes while the lid is on, because the air pressure pushing on the side of the bottle is stronger than the downward pull of gravity on the water. But when the lid is removed, air rushes in and adds its force to gravity's pull...and SPLASH!

MARBLE MADNESS

This is another experiment that can be performed as a magic trick. Tell your family and friends that you are going to pick up a marble in a cup without touching the marble.

Step 1

You will need a wine glass shaped like this.

This part is the bowl. It needs to be wider in the middle than at the rim.

Step 2

Ask a volunteer if they can pick up a marble in the glass without using the glass to scoop it up, or touching it. They won't be able to!

Step 3

Now show them how it's done. Place the glass over the marble. Hold the glass by the base and start gently moving it in a circular motion.

Step 4

The marble should start rolling around inside the glass.

Step 5

Rolling the marble at the right speed should keep it rotating in the widest part of the bowl. Lift the glass up as you rotate it. Your audience will impressed!

HOW DOES IT WORK?

This experiment is a contest between two forces: gravity and centrifugal force. As long as the marble is rolling fast enough, the centrifugal force pushing it outward to the widest part of the glass will be greater than the gravity pulling it downward. So the marble will roll around the glass rather than dropping out.

This really puts a new spin on gravity!

BALANCING BUTTERFLY

Is it possible to balance a piece of paper on a single finger? Sure it is! Here's how to make a beautiful, balancing butterfly.

Step 1

Draw a butterfly shape on a piece of thin cardboard. The tips of the wings must be above the head.

Step 2

Ink over the lines with a black marker. Decorate the body and wings with colored pens or paints.

Step 3

Cut out the shape with scissors.

Step 4

Fix matching coins to the tips of the wings.

Step 5

Bend the wings down a little.

Step 6

The balance point should be near the head, depending on the weight of your coins and the cardboard thickness.

Step 7

You should be able to balance the butterfly on the tip of your finger!

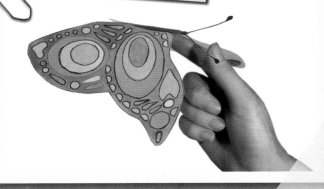

Step 8

You can put butterflies all around the room, on furniture, mirrors, ornaments, flower pots—wherever there's a place for them to balance!

These butterflies make great decorations!

HOW DOES IT WORK?

When the coin weights are added to the butterfly, the center of gravity falls almost directly between them, which is where your finger is, so it makes it easy to balance.

HOMEMADE COMPASS

You will never be lost again once you know how to make your own compass!

YOU WILL NEED:

★ A glass

★ Water

★ A sewing needle (be careful of the point!)

★ Thin cardboard

★ Scissors

★ A pencil

★ Colored markers

★ A bar magnet

Step 1

Hold a needle in one hand and stroke the north end of a magnet along its length 50 times, from point to eye.

Make strokes like this.

Step 2

Using scissors, cut a piece of thin cardboard in an arrow shape, just a little longer than your needle.

Step 3

Thread the needle through the thin cardboard, making sure the point is at the same end as the arrow.

Step 4

Fill a glass with water.

Step 5

Gently lower the arrow onto the water.

Step 6

The arrow should point north!

If the arrow is pointing south, you may have used the wrong end of the magnet in step 1!

Step 7

Now that you know which direction is north, write all the compass points on a piece of cardboard, just a little larger than your glass.

HOW DOES IT WORK?

When you rub the needle with the magnet, it becomes a weak magnet itself and will automatically point to the magnetic north pole. Floating it on the water reduces the friction, allowing the needle to easily turn around to point in the direction it is attracted to.

Now that we have a compass, we just need a treasure map!

Place your glass on top of this card.

WOBBLER TOY

This wobbler toy makes a great gift! No matter how much it wobbles, it will never fall down.

YOU WILL NEED:

★ Table tennis ball

★ Scissors

★ A piece of paper

★ A ruler

★ A pencil

★ Colored markers

★ Tape

★ Modeling clay

★ A gluestick

Step 1

Get an adult to help you cut a table tennis ball in half, using scissors.

Step 2

Cut out a rectangle of paper measuring 5 x 2 inches (125 x 50 mm). Draw a line half an inch (12 mm) from one narrow end.

If you push them over, they bounce right back!

Step 3

Draw a face and body on the paper, like this. We're going to decorate this one as a fairy, but there are other ideas on page 18.

Step 4

Roll the paper into a tube, overlapping as far as the pencil line. Fix it in place with the gluestick.

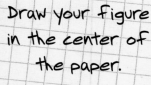

Draw your figure in the center of the paper.

Step 5

Tape one half of the ball to each end. Finish drawing the top of the head.

Step 6

She won't stand up yet!

Step 7

Take the foot end off. Put a lump of modeling clay in the middle of the half ball and and stick it back on the body.

Step 8

Now stand your character up, and try pushing it over.

Step 9

You could make more wobblers and decorate them as aliens or circus performers, or use your own ideas!

Gravity pulls DOWN, but it makes wobblers stand UP!

HOW DOES IT WORK?

The wobbler has a very low center of gravity, because its top half is light but the base is heavy. When another force acts on it (for example, when you give it a push), gravity will pull it back to a point directly above the point where its mass is concentrated. This is called its state of equilibrium.

PARACHUTE JUMP

It's time to parachute some cork commandos behind enemy lines. Which parachute works best?

YOU WILL NEED:

★ String

★ Materials for making the parachutes, such as plastic shopping bags, paper, foil, and tissue paper

★ A ruler

★ Scissors

★ A pencil

★ Tape

★ A cork

★ A small eyehook

★ A kitchen scale

★ A sturdy chair

★ A stopwatch (on a cell phone or wristwatch)

Step 1

Using scissors, cut a 12 inch (30 cm) square from a plastic shopping bag.

Step 2

Cut four pieces of string 12 inches (30 cm) long. Tie one end of each piece of string to a corner of the square of plastic.

Step 3

Twist an eyehook into one end of a cork.

Step 4

Hold the strings from the parachute together, and tie them to the screw.

Step 5

Stand on a chair, reach as high as you can, and drop the parachute.

Ask a friend to time how long the cork takes to fall!

Step 6

Try making parachutes of different sizes and materials. You can also try using other objects as weights, such as plastic toys. Drop them from the same height.

Step 7

Make a chart to see which features make the best parachutes. Time your test drops. Measure the size and weight of the parachute.

Size	Weight	Material	Time

HOW DOES IT WORK?

Parachutes work by creating air resistance. This is a kind of friction which works against the pull of gravity. The best way to increase air resistance is by making as large a surface area as possible. So the size of your parachute will probably make more of a difference than anything else.

RUBBER BAND RACERS

YOU WILL NEED:

- ★ A spool (with no thread)
- ★ A pencil
- ★ A candle
- ★ A skewer
- ★ Rubber bands
- ★ Tape
- ★ Colored markers
- ★ A paperclip
- ★ A craft knife

Create you own lean, mean racing machine with a simple motor. Then find a friend to race against. Ready, set, GO!

Step 1

Hook a paper clip onto a rubber band. Then thread the band through the hole in a cotton spool.

Step 2

Twist one end of the paper clip inside the spool so that it cannot turn.

If you have a wooden spool, fix the paper clip with tape.

Step 3

Ask an adult to help you cut a slice of candle about half an inch (1 cm) wide, then make a hole in it with a skewer.

Step 4

Thread the rubber band through the piece of candle.

Turn the pencil around until it won't go any farther.

Step 5

Pass a pencil through the rubber band and wind it up.

Step 6

Put it on a flat surface and let go!

Step 7

Decorate your racers and test them against each other! You could try different ideas to improve your racers. For example, what happens if you use a shorter pencil?

Now it's time to race against your pals!

HOW DOES IT WORK?

Winding up the rubber band creates a store of potential energy. When you let the racer go, the band unwinds and the potential energy turns into kinetic energy. Va-va-voom!

BALLOON MONSTER

This party game uses the power of static electricity to create a whole lot of fun and laughter.

YOU WILL NEED:

★ As many balloons as possible
★ Some friends!

Step 1

Blow up plenty of balloons.

Step 2

Decide who's going to be the first to take their turn as the "balloon monster."

Step 3

The first player rubs a balloon on their hair, and sticks it on the "monster."

Step 4

All the players take turns in putting a balloon on the "monster."

Step 5

Keep going until a balloon (or several balloons) falls off.

Step 6

Whoever was playing when a balloon fell off becomes the new "monster."

Step 7

The game starts again!

Step 8

Keep a record for the most balloons you can get on one person.

That sure is a LOT of balloons!!

Step 9

Whoever placed the last balloon that "stuck," in the round with the most balloons, wins the game.

+ Positive charge

— Negative charge

HOW DOES IT WORK?

Rubbing balloons against your hair gives them a negative charge. That's because some of the electrons—tiny, negatively charged particles—in your hair will rub off onto the balloon. When you hold the balloon against clothes, the electrons on the surface of the clothes move away from the negatively charged balloon. That makes the surface positively charged— and attracted to the balloon.

SLED VS. GO-KART

One of mankind's greatest inventions is the wheel. It's also one of the most fun! Find out why in this experiment.

YOU WILL NEED

★ Corrugated cardboard (could be cut from a box)

★ Tape

★ An unopened can

★ Four spools without thread

★ Mounting putty

★ Two pencils of the same length

★ A ruler

★ An old ballpoint pen (for scoring cardboard)

★ A flat tray or board

★ A protractor

Step 1

Cut two squares of corrugated cardboard, with sides the same length as the pencils.

Step 2

Rule a line 1.5 inches (4 cm) from opposite sides of a piece of cardboard. Score along the lines with an old pen, and fold the sides up to make a tray shape. Do this twice.

Step 3

Set one tray aside. This is now a sled.

Step 4

Take the other tray, turn it over and attach two pencils with tape.

The pencils have become axles.

Step 5

Turn it over again and put four spools on the ends of the pencils. Stop them falling off with blobs of mounting putty.

Step 6

Stick a can in the sled with tape. Then place the sled at one end of a flat tray or board.

Which will move the first, the go-Kart or the sled?

Step 7

Slowly tilt the tray. Measure the angle of the slope when the sled starts moving.

Step 8

Repeat the experiment with the go-kart.

Step 9

Check the angle when the go-kart starts moving.

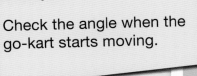

HOW DOES IT WORK?

In this experiment, the force of gravity is being resisted by friction. For the sled to move, it must overcome the friction on the whole of its bottom surface. However the go-kart is able to easily move, because its wheels reduce the friction by making it able to roll.

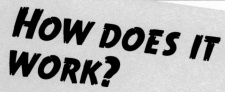

29

GLOSSARY

air pressure
(EHR PREH-shur) The force of air as it pushes on things.

air resistance
(EHR rih-ZIS-tens) A type of friction that slows an object's movement through the air.

center of gravity
(SEN-tur UV GRA-vih-tee) The point that marks the center of an object's mass, so that it acts as a balancing point.

centrifugal force
(sen-TRIH-fuh-guhl FORS) The force that seems to draw a rotating object away from the center of rotation.

charge (CHAHRJ) The description of whether an object has a balanced or unbalanced amount of electrons.

electron (ih-LEK-tron) A tiny particle that has a negative charge.

equilibrium
(ee-kwih-LIB-ree-um) Balanced between two or more objects or forces.

friction (FRIK-shun) A force that slows moving objects.

gravity (GRAV-it-ee) A force of attraction between the mass of two objects.

kinetic energy
(kin-ET-ik EN-er-jee) The energy that moving objects use.

mass (MAS) The amount of basic particles that an object has, which on Earth also indicates how heavy that object is.

potential energy
(puh-TEN-shul EH-nur-jee) Energy that an object has stored.

static electricity
(STA-tik ih-lek-TRIH-suh-tee) An electrical charge that builds up, usually because of friction.

terminal velocity
(TUR-muh-nul veh-LO-suh-tee) The greatest speed that a falling object reaches.

Oh, so THAT's what that word means!

FURTHER READING

Brallier, Jess and Robert Andrew Parker. *Who Was Albert Einstein?* New York: Grosset & Dunlap, 2002.

Brasch, Nicolas. *Tricks of Sound and Light.* The Science Behind. Mankato, MN: Smart Apple Media, 2011.

Challoner, Jack. *DK Eyewitness Books: Energy.* New York: DK Children, 2012.

Connolly, Sean. *The Book of Potentially Catastrophic Science: 50 Experiments for Daring Young Scientists.* New York: Workman Publishing, 2010.

Green, Dan and Simon Basher. *Physics: Why Matter Matters!* New York: Kingfisher Press, 2011.

Lepora, Nathan. *Twists and Turns: Forces in Motion.* The Science Behind Thrill Rides. New York: Gareth Stevens Publishing, 2008.

Mercer, Bobby. *The Flying Machine Book: Build and Launch 35 Rockets, Gliders, Helicopters, Boomerangs, and More.* Chicago, IL: Chicago Review Press, 2012.

Silverman, Buffy. *Stop and Go, Fast and Slow: Moving Objects In Different Ways.* Vero Beach, FL: Rourke Publishing Group, 2011.

Slade, Suzanne. *Cool Physics Activities for Girls.* Mankato, MN: Capstone Press, 2012.

Websites

For web resources related to the subject of this book, go to: www.windmillbooks.com/weblinks and select this book's title.

INDEX